GREATEST MOVIE MONSTERS

KING KONG
AND OTHER MONSTROUS APES

JENNIFER WAY

rosen publishing's
rosen
central®

Published in 2016 by The Rosen Publishing Group, Inc.
29 East 21st Street, New York, NY 10010

Library of Congress Cataloging-in-Publication Data

Way, Jennifer.
King Kong and other monstrous apes/Jennifer Way.—First edition.
     pages cm.—(Greatest movie monsters)
Includes bibliographical references and index.
ISBN 978-1-4994-3537-5 (library bound) — ISBN 978-1-4994-3539-9 (pbk.) —
ISBN 978-1-4994-3540-5 (6-pack)
1. King Kong films—History and criticism. 2. King Kong (Fictitious character) I. Title.
PN1995.9.K55W39 2016
791.43'75—dc23

2014047236

Manufactured in the United States of America

On the cover: Starring a fierce-looking Kong (played by English actor Andy Serkis)— *King Kong*, directed, co-written, and produced by Peter Jackson in 2005—is a remake of the eponymous 1933 film.

THE ORIGIN OF KONG

A huge, angry ape is climbing up the outside of the Empire State Building in New York City, clutching a screaming woman. Airplanes are circling the ape, trying to shoot him down. This scene from the climax of *King Kong* is so well-known that it is familiar even to people who have never seen the movie!

Upon its premiere in 1933, *King Kong* captured people's imaginations and

The iconic scene of King Kong swatting at biplanes from atop the Empire State Building in the classic 1933 movie is burned into moviegoers' minds.

became an instant classic. The special effects used in the movie introduced new ways for filmmakers to bring monsters to the silver screen. The character of King Kong became famous as one of Hollywood's greatest movie monsters, spawning sequels and remakes as well as inspiring numerous other movies about monstrous apes.

King Kong brought together several things that were popular with movie audiences in the 1920s and early 1930s. People loved seeing films that showed exotic locations and animals in the wild,

ACTUALITIES AND JUNGLE FILMS

The writers and director of *King Kong* were influenced not just by fictional "jungle films," but by "actualities," which was what documentaries were called at the time. Actualities were filmed in exotic locations around the world and featured the indigenous people and the animals native to that place. A few popular actualities and jungle films from that time include *Bali, the Unknown: Or Ape Island* (1921), *Nanook of the North* (1922), *Man Hunt* (1926), *Chang* (1927), and *Rango* (1931).

Rango **is a jungle film that details the adventures of native Sumatrans and orangutans living in the rain forest. The director, Ernest B. Schoedsack, would go on to codirect** King Kong.

regardless of whether the movies were documentaries or fantasy. *King Kong* shows lots of mythical and prehistoric animals on a wild, fictional island. *King Kong* is also an example of the popular "jungle movie" genre of the time. In these types of movies, a scientist or explorer goes to a faraway or uncharted place to test a theory or solve a mystery and ends up finding monstrous creatures or animals thought to be extinct. It is safe to say the characters in *King Kong* find a bit more ape than they can handle!

THE LOST WORLD AND CREATING KONG

The most famous jungle movie was *The Lost World*. This 1925 silent film was directed by Harry O. Hoyt and written by Marion Fairfax, based on the book by Sir Arthur Conan Doyle. (Doyle is most famous for having created legendary fictional detective Sherlock Holmes.) This story is about a scientist who leads an expedition from London, England, to a remote part of South America where he believes dinosaurs still roam the land. They find many prehistoric creatures and bring back one dinosaur to London, where it runs wild before disappearing. Like other jungle movies, *The Lost World* shows audiences that the modern world is still full of mysteries.

The Lost World featured stop-motion animation by Willis O'Brien. Stop-motion animation is a special effect in which models are posed and filmed frame by frame to create the illusion that the models are moving. O'Brien used this technique in *The Lost World* to make it look as though dinosaurs were roaming in a remote jungle. O'Brien would use similar settings, creatures, and special-effects techniques again in *King Kong*.

   King Kong brought together a group of writers, actors, two directors, and a special-effects team to create a movie unlike anything that had ever been seen before. They worked for months on location and on sets at the movie studio lot to create the world of *King Kong*. Chapter 2 will explain in detail the filming of the original movies.

Willis O'Brien brought the stop-motion animation skills he honed creating dinosaur action sequences in The Lost World (1925) to the production of King Kong.

A KONG FOR EVERY ERA

At first glance it might seem that the King Kong character is all monster and nothing more, and in some movies that is all he is. In other King Kong movies, however, the ape's familiar, humanlike features encourage the audience to see past his monstrous surface, and in some movies he can be viewed as something of a tragic figure. Much of how the King Kong character is interpreted depends on how well the special effects used to create the ape allow him to interact with human actors and show emotion. *King Kong* has been remade twice. It was first remade in 1976, with a sequel called *King Kong Lives* in 1986. It was remade once again in 2005. Japan's Toho Studios also added the King Kong character to its stable of movie monsters in the 1960s. Chapter 3 will explain in detail the reboots and reimaginings King Kong has experienced.

AN INSPIRING APE

King Kong is not the only monstrous ape in the movies. His popularity inspired other Hollywood movies, such as *White Pongo* (1945), *Mighty Joe Young* (1949), and *Congo* (1995). You can also see King Kong's influence in many cheaply made B movies with monstrous apes, such as *The Ape Man* (1943), *Konga* (1961), and *The Mighty Gorga* (1969). Even the *Planet of the Apes* movies of the 1960s and the 2000s should raise a paw in thanks to *King Kong* for being the original movie to make people go ape for apes. Chapter 4 will explore some of the movies that *King Kong* inspired and Kong's effect on pop culture as a whole.

Aside from all of these monstrous ape movies, *King Kong* laid the foundation for moviegoers' love of special effects–driven adventures. Willis O'Brien's pioneering effects were used in other movies, were developed further, and led to ever more sophisticated filmmaking techniques. You can see this pursuit of cutting-edge effects in the fantasy, science fiction, and horror movies that audiences flock to nearly one hundred years later, such as *Gravity* (2013) or *Godzilla* (2014).

KING KONG AND SON OF KONG

ovies are a collaborative art, meaning it takes the work of many people to create a film. *King Kong* was no exception. There was a team of people involved in every part of its production: from its script to its special effects to its cast of actors and its pair of directors. This chapter will explain how all of those elements came together for the original movies.

THE *KING KONG* STORYLINES

The story of *King Kong* started with an idea by Merian C. Cooper. He assigned screenwriter and best-selling author Edgar Wallace to write the script. Wallace started the script but died before he could finish it. Cooper then hired James Creelman to write the script and later brought in Ruth Rose to clean up and tighten the script, since it involved work from different writers. The script was still being worked on as the movie was being shot, so in some scenes the actors improvised their dialogue!

King Kong is about a filmmaker named Carl Denham (played by Robert Armstrong) who sails with a film crew and actress Ann Darrow (Fay Wray) to the mysterious Skull Island to make a movie. Denham tells the crew about a legendary ape called Kong that is supposed to live there. After the movie crew reaches Skull Island, the inhabitants of the island kidnap Darrow and present her to King Kong.

Denham and his crew go after King Kong to rescue Darrow. During the mission to rescue her, Denham and his crew see that other huge creatures—including dinosaurs—live on the island. A dinosaur nearly kills Darrow, but King Kong saves her. This hints

EFTER EN IDÉ AV
EDGAR WALLACE OCH **MERIAN COOPER**
MED
ROBERT ARMSTRONG, FAY WRAY, BRUCE CABOT OCH **KONG**
VÄRLDENS ÅTTONDE UNDERVERK.

This is the poster for the original King Kong, *which shows the dramatic Empire State Building scene.*

to her (and to the movie audience) that King Kong is capable of feelings despite his violent actions and his monstrous appearance.

Denham manages to capture King Kong and brings him back to New York City. There, King Kong is chained up and put on display as the "Eighth Wonder of the World." King Kong escapes, captures Darrow, and climbs up the Empire State Building holding her. He brings Darrow to safety but is shot down by airplanes circling the skyscraper, and he falls to his death.

Son of Kong was written by Ruth Rose. The story picks up soon after the events of *King Kong*. Carl Denham (again played by Robert Armstrong) is facing legal problems from the destruction caused by King Kong's rampage in New York City. He sails away with Captain Englehorn (Frank Reicher), who commands the ship that brought Denham to Skull Island in the earlier film.

During their travels, the men meet a singer named Hilda (Helen Mack) as well as Nils Helstrom (John Marston), who had earlier sold Denham the map to Skull Island. Helstrom claims that there is treasure on the island. Intrigued, the three men and Hilda sail to Skull Island.

Once there, Denham discovers that the inhabitants of the island blame him for the destruction King Kong caused to their village. The four travelers leave the island's inhabitants and then Hilda and Denham meet and befriend a large albino gorilla. Denham believes the ape is King Kong's son and names him Little Kong. Denham and company fight more dinosaurs and other oversized creatures and are helped by Little Kong, who eventually dies saving them. Denham does indeed find the Skull Island treasure, and the surviving members of his party split the money.

GETTING STARTED

Merian C. Cooper had wanted to make a movie with apes ever since he had traveled to Africa to film *The Four Feathers* (1929). He dreamed up the basic idea that would become *King Kong* soon after. His earliest notion involved filming animals on locations in Africa and Asia and then combining that with studio footage with actors. Paramount Pictures turned down this idea as too expensive.

Cooper moved on to filming *The Most Dangerous Game* (1932) for RKO, a motion picture company that was big in the first half of the 1900s. A large jungle set had been built for the movie. Around this time, Cooper had also seen some of Willis O'Brien's stop-motion animation. That gave Cooper an idea. He could reuse the jungle set instead of filming on location. Then he could have O'Brien create models and use stop-motion animation instead of animals. He would also cast actors he already knew from *The Most Dangerous Game* and even film parts of both movies at the same time. Cooper presented this idea to RKO, and the studio gave him the green light to write the script and film the movie. The budget for *King Kong* was about $600,000, which is about $11 million in 2014 dollars.

Merian C. Cooper and Ernest B. Schoedsack chose Robert Armstrong and Fay Wray to be the leads in **King Kong** *because the directors had worked with these actors before.*

THE CAST

Cooper and Ernest B. Schoedsack, his co-director, cast *King Kong* using two actors they had worked with before. Fay Wray had appeared in their films *The Four Feathers* and *The Most Dangerous Game* before being cast as Ann Darrow. She would go on to star in dozens of other movies, but *King Kong* would be the movie for which she was most remembered.

Robert Armstrong, who had also starred in *The Most Dangerous Game*, was chosen to play Carl Denham. Bruce Cabot made one of his earliest screen appearances as Jack Driscoll, and experienced stage actor Frank Reicher rounded out the main cast as Captain Englehorn. Armstrong and Reicher would later play their roles again in *Son of Kong*.

FILMING *KING KONG*

Cooper and Shoedsack were codirectors, but that did not mean they worked together on every scene. As the two men had different working styles and skills, they filmed different types of scenes. Cooper would direct the scenes that used miniatures and other special effects because he had the patience and eye for detail that these scenes needed. Schoedsack would direct the live-action scenes because he was better at keeping those scenes moving at a brisk pace.

King Kong was filmed over an eight-month period from May 1932 to January 1933. Cooper started by filming jungle scenes on the set left over from *The Most Dangerous Game*. Next Schoedsack filmed location shots in New York City. These were outdoor establishing shots that showed the city as well as shots that would be used later as background projections for the Empire State Building set.

Then the directors shot beach scenes on location in San Pedro, California, and Skull Island village scenes and interior scenes on the RKO lot in Culver City, California. They also used the Shrine Auditorium in Los Angeles for the scenes of King Kong on display as the "Eighth Wonder of the World." Finally, they filmed the special-effects shots.

After filming was completed, the directors edited the movie to a 100-minute running time. Then they added Kong's roars, which were a mix of lion and tiger roars played backward. The finishing touch was Max Steiner's score, music that added another exciting element to the film.

SPECTACULAR SPECIAL EFFECTS

Special effects are the backbone not just to the look of *King Kong* but to the plot itself. Before Cooper met special-effects master O'Brien, he planned to make his movie by filming a gorilla and some Komodo dragons and using whatever footage he got. Then Cooper met O'Brien, and the two began working together on a dinosaur movie called *Creation* for RKO. O'Brien was creating stop-motion footage for the film, but he was not happy with the story. Cooper was impressed with O'Brien's footage, but he suggested to the studio that *Creation* be canceled because it would be too expensive. However, Cooper decided that O'Brien's stop-motion animation techniques would allow him to make the epic monstrous ape picture he wanted to make in a studio.

Willis O'Brien's special-effects techniques allowed him to create different worlds within his studio using clay models, stop-motion animation, miniatures, matte background paintings, and back projection. He had devised many of his techniques working on *The Lost World*, and in the years between that film and *King Kong* he had perfected his methods. O'Brien even adapted some of his signature scenes from *The Lost World* to *King Kong*. For example, Kong rampages through New York City like a dinosaur does in London in *The Lost World*.

King Kong himself was an 18-inch-tall (46-centimeter) puppet made from aluminum, rubber, and rabbit fur designed by O'Brien and built by Marcel Delgado. This was the model that was filmed using stop-motion animation as well as in the long, full shots of the ape. For tighter shots, such as when King Kong is holding Ann Darrow, O'Brien and his team built large arms, hands, and feet using steel, rubber, wood, and fur. They also built a large head of rubber and aluminum that had controls a crew member stood inside and operated. These controls created King Kong's facial expressions in close-ups.

To create illusions like King Kong climbing the Empire State Building, O'Brien and his team built miniature buildings

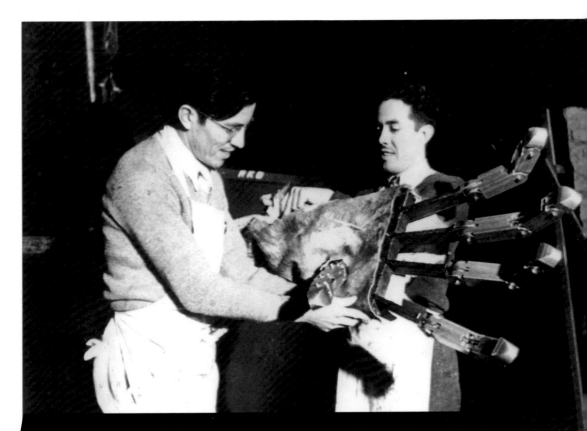

Willis O'Brien and his team built large, movable mechanical body parts like the hand shown here. The parts were used for close-up shots of the ape in **King Kong.**

that made the ape look as though it were 50 feet (15 meters) tall. They also used traveling mattes to make studio shots look as though they had been filmed outside and rear projections to combine shots of the actors with the models. All of these techniques came together to create the look of the film. Whether a technique had been developed or perfected by O'Brien and his team, the combined number of effects used in *King Kong* set a new standard for movie special effects and made the film an instant classic.

A CLASSIC AND ITS SEQUEL

King Kong was released in March 1933. This was during the height of the Great Depression. Millions of people were out

WILLIS O'BRIEN

Willis O'Brien was not the first person to use special effects in film, and he built on techniques created by earlier filmmakers. Georges Méliès was an early pioneer in special effects in late nineteenth- and early twentieth-century France. He perfected the use of effects such as multiple exposures, time-lapse photography, and editing to create magical films. His best-known film is the 1902 short *A Trip to the Moon*.

of work—would they spend what little money they had to see a movie about a monstrous ape? They certainly did: the monster movie became a monster hit.

The reviews for *King Kong* were generally good, and in particular reviewers praised the film's technical achievements. For example, the *New York Times* called the whole movie "fantastic," while *Variety* magazine noted the similarities between the movie and *The Lost World* but said *King Kong* was

In this scene from **Son of Kong,** *the younger Kong fights a dinosaur.*

the better made, more exciting movie of the two. The *Variety* reviewer also said that although the plot was silly and the acting was not great, it was the spectacle of the filmmaking that held the greatest appeal.

King Kong made about $2 million in its initial release in the spring of 1933, which is about $37 million in 2014 dollars. This was considered a success, and a sequel, *Son of Kong*, was rushed into production and released in December 1933. The sequel's hurried creation led to it being a poorly received follow-up. *Son of Kong* received mostly bad reviews and made only about $600,000, roughly $11 million in 2014 dollars.

The yearly Academy Awards have honored achievements in filmmaking since 1929. *King Kong*, however, was not nominated for any Academy Awards. One reason is that at the time there were no categories to honor special effects. *King Kong* has garnered greater recognition over the years. In 1975, the American Film Institute named it one of the fifty best American films. The Library of Congress named *King Kong* as a historically significant film in 1991 and selected it for preservation by the United States National Film Registry. These honors cemented *King Kong*'s place in both pop culture and film history.

CHAPTER 3

KING KONG REBOOTS AND OTHER APPEARANCES

The *King Kong* story and its main character are timeless. The character of King Kong has appeared with other monsters in movies produced in Japan in the 1960s. As noted earlier, the original *King Kong* movie has been remade twice. The first, from 1976, even had a sequel in 1986. The second remake of *King Kong*, directed by Peter Jackson in 2005, was a modern special-effects blockbuster, much like the original had been when it was first released.

TOHO STUDIOS' MOVIES

In the 1960s, Japan's Toho Studios made two movies with King Kong as its star. They were *King Kong vs. Godzilla* (1962) and *King Kong Escapes* (1967).

Around 1960, Willis O'Brien had an idea for a movie in which Kong would fight another monster. He shopped his idea to different Hollywood movie studios, but he was told it would be too expensive to do the stop-motion animation. Producer John Beck took O'Brien's idea to Toho Studios. The studio reworked the idea to have King Kong fight Godzilla.

Because stop-motion animation was too expensive, the Toho Studios production used models and puppets of the monsters for some scenes. For other scenes, "suitimation" was used. This meant that actors in monster suits moved around on sets with miniature buildings and scenery, creating the illusion of big monsters stomping around. The suitimation actors based their moves on those of professional wrestlers!

These crude-looking methods fit in with the lighter tone that special-effects director Eiji Tsuburaya desired. He wanted the series to appeal to kids, so he did things to add humor to the action. For example, he shows Godzilla and King Kong tossing a boulder back and forth as though they are tossing a beach ball.

An American production team edited the Toho

This scene from King Kong Escapes *shows Kong throwing a boulder at his attackers. The Toho Studios Kong films were light, campy monster movies aimed at young audiences.*

movies for their American releases. The dialogue was redubbed in English, and scenes were cut or moved. For *King Kong vs. Godzilla*, they even filmed and added in a newscaster who commented on the movie's action!

In *King Kong vs. Godzilla*, Mr. Tako (Ichirô Arishima) sends people to a mysterious island to bring back proof of the giant ape King Kong. They find and capture Kong. However, he escapes and swims to Japan. Elsewhere, a submarine breaks an iceberg that had trapped Godzilla, who escapes and goes to Japan. There, King Kong and Godzilla fight each other.

In *King Kong Escapes*, a mad scientist and an evil mastermind build a robot King Kong called Mechni-Kong to dig for the radioactive Element X at the North Pole. When the Mechni-Kong is not up to the job, they decide to kidnap King Kong. They also kidnap Lt. Susan Watson (Linda Miller), whom Kong has befriended. Eventually Kong escapes, swims to Japan, and successfully battles Mechni-Kong, defeating the mad scientist and evil mastermind's plans for good.

WHO'S THE HERO?

There were rumors that *King Kong vs. Godzilla* had two different endings, with Godzilla winning in the Japanese version and losing in the American version. This myth is not true, though. At the time the Toho Studios King Kong films were made, the Godzilla character was a villain, so King Kong was the hero in both versions.

The Toho Studios monster movies featured often-clumsy dialogue and many a monster playfully fighting and wreaking havoc. The flimsiness of the stories combined with some clumsy editing between the miniatures and full-size shots, as well as bad dubbing of English, earned these movies generally poor reviews, although many people enjoy them for their silly, campy fun.

THE DE LAURENTIIS KING KONG MOVIES

Movie producer Dino De Laurentiis remade *King Kong* in 1976 and produced a sequel called *King Kong Lives* in 1986. For both films, John Guillermin was the director and Carlo Rambaldi fashioned the creature designs. The designs included suits and several varied mechanical masks. Rambaldi used multiple mechanical masks that gave his Kong the widest range of facial expressions that had yet been seen. Rambaldi also built a 40-foot-tall (12-m) mechanical King Kong for the first movie. It cost more than $1 million to build, but because the effects team did not think it looked convincing, it can be seen in only a few brief shots in *King Kong*.

The story for *King Kong* was based on the 1933 script, but screenwriter Lorenzo Semple Jr. updated the settings and characters, aiming for a lighter tone. In this version, Fred Wilson (Charles Grodin) leads an expedition to a mysterious island in search of oil. Jack Prescott (Jeff Bridges) is a scientist who goes along to research a mythic ape. Along the way, the crew picks up Dwan (Jessica Lange), an actress who has been lost at sea. As in the original movie, they find King Kong on the island and bring him back to New York City and put him on display. Kong breaks free and goes on a rampage, this time climbing the World Trade Center before his fatal fall.

King Kong received mixed reviews. Critics who praised the movie enjoyed the light tone. Critics who wrote negative reviews thought it was too silly. The film was a commercial success, though. It was also honored with three Academy Awards: Best Visual Effects, Best Cinematography, and Best Sound.

The 1976 King Kong *was based on the original movie but was updated. One big change was the climactic scene, which took place atop the World Trade Center instead of the Empire State Building, as shown in this poster for the movie.*

The general success of *King Kong* inspired De Laurentiis to make the sequel *King Kong Lives*. Steven Pressman wrote the script. In this movie, we learn that King Kong did not die at the end of *King Kong* but has been in a coma for the last ten years. Dr. Amy Franklin (Linda Hamilton) wants to operate on Kong but needs blood from another giant ape to do it. A team searches for and captures one, whom they name Lady Kong. After the successful operation, King Kong and Lady Kong escape. The pair are chased by the army, and Kong is fatally wounded, but he manages to say good-bye to Lady Kong and their newborn before dying. Although it was marketed in much the same way as the earlier movie, *King Kong Lives* received bad reviews and was a box-office flop.

PETER JACKSON'S *KING KONG* (2005)

Director Peter Jackson fell in love with the 1933 version of *King Kong* when he was nine years old. He dreamed of one day remaking his favorite movie to recapture the spectacle of the original using state-of-the-art special effects. After he finished directing the *Lord of the Rings* movies, his wish came true.

Jackson's version of *King Kong* closely follows the 1933 original. It was written by Jackson, Fran Walsh, and Philippa Boyens and swells the movie's length to three hours from the original's one hundred minutes. It stars Naomi Watts as Ann Darrow, Jack Black as Carl Denham, Adrien Brody as Jack Driscoll, and Andy Serkis as King Kong.

King Kong was filmed mostly on soundstages in New Zealand. Jackson created the worlds of Skull Island and 1930s New York City by building miniatures and using green screens so that backgrounds or other details could be added after filming was done.

The most important special effect used in the movie was the motion-capture technology used to record Andy Serkis's movements. This technique required putting special sensors on Serkis's face and body. The sensors recorded his movements. These recordings were then played back on a computer so that digital-effects artists could use them to animate Kong's movements.

Serkis was experienced with doing motion capture because he had done it before as Gollum in Jackson's *Lord of the*

Peter Jackson, the director of the 2005 King Kong *film, holds a skeleton of a stop-motion Kong puppet that was designed by Willis O'Brien for the 1933 movie.*

Peter Jackson's **King Kong** *hewed closely to the original, adding dazzling special effects. However, Andy Serkis's emotional, motion-captured performance as Kong might have been the* **best** *special effect.*

Rings movies. For *King Kong*, Serkis studied ape movements and used a voice box he called the Kongalizer so that he could look and sound as apelike as possible.

Reviews for Jackson's *King Kong* were largely positive. His use of special effects impressed critics. His motion-captured Kong was singled out for his ability to connect with the audience and the actors. The movie was a box-office success and went on to win three Academy Awards: Best Visual Effects, Best Sound Mixing, and Best Sound Editing.

KING KONG AND MONSTROUS APES IN POP CULTURE

King Kong has reared his furry head not just in movies but on television, in comic books, and even on the stage! He is not the only monstrous ape out there, either. King Kong's enduring popularity has inspired other Hollywood movies about fearsome primates, as well as countless campy B movies. This chapter will explore some of King Kong's nonmovie outings and introduce you to other monstrous ape movies you might enjoy seeking out.

KING KONG ON TV

King Kong has been made into a television show two times. The first was *King Kong*, a cartoon series that was produced in Japan and aired in that country as well as in the United States. The show had twenty-five episodes and ran for three seasons, from 1966 to 1969.

King Kong includes characters from the 1933 movie, the Toho Studios movies, and characters that are original to

The 1998 Mighty Joe Young *remake starred Charlize Theron as Jill and Bill Paxton as Greg O'Hara.*

the show. In this series, King Kong befriends the Bond family and they have adventures in which they save the world from monsters, aliens, and mad scientists, as well as other bad guys. Today, only the first season of the show is available on DVD.

Kong: The Animated Series was the second King Kong television show. This cartoon had one forty-episode season from 2000 to 2001. This show follows the King Kong story after his fall from the Empire State Building. A doctor creates a new King Kong by cloning the fallen Kong. This new Kong is brought back to Kong Island. Years later, the doctor's grandson goes to the island. There he and Kong work together to stop a mad scientist from taking over the world. Today the full series is available on DVD. There are also two direct-to-DVD movies based on the series, *Kong: King of Atlantis* (2005) and *Kong: Return to the Jungle* (2007).

KONG IN COMICS AND ON STAGE

A fantasy beast such as King Kong is a natural fit for comic books. It is not surprising then, that Kong has had many outings in this medium. For example, the 1960s cartoon series *King Kong* had ministories appear in comic magazines in the United States and Japan.

In 1968, Merian C. Cooper commissioned Gold Key Comics to put out a comic version of the 1932 novelization of King Kong by Delos W. Lovelace. This comic was successful and was reprinted when the 1976 version of *King Kong* was released.

In 1991, Monster Comics put out a six-issue comic adaptation of *King Kong*. This rendition was also based on Lovelace's novelization and includes extra scenes that were not in the 1933 film.

In 2004, Dark Horse Comics published an illustrated novel called *Kong: King of Skull Island*. This novel by Joe DeVito was a sequel to *King Kong* created with the permission of Merian C. Cooper's estate. The following year, Dark Horse Comics also produced comics to tie in with the release of Peter Jackson's *King Kong*. The company had originally intended to create a three-comic miniseries, but after the first issue was published it combined all three issues as a paperback collection.

King Kong is truly a star of both stage and screen. In 2013, a musical version of *King Kong* premiered in Australia. This giant production uses a 20-foot-tall (6-m) animatronic ape to

The Kong in the 2013 Australian musical King Kong *was designed by the Creature Technology Company. The show was praised for its spectacular use of technology and design.*

portray King Kong. The show was based on the 1933 film and included songs from the 1930s as well as original tunes.

OTHER MONSTROUS APE MOVIES

King Kong has been reimagined many times over the years. This great ape is also the inspiration for all kinds of monstrous ape movies. Some of these films are slick Hollywood productions while other movies are built for cheap thrills, proving there's an ape for every audience and for every budget!

Mighty Joe Young was a 1949 RKO film about Jill Young (Terry Moore), who lives in Tanzania and has raised a gorilla named Joe. Joe is about 12 feet (4 m) tall, which is about twice the size of a normal gorilla. Young is persuaded by an American nightclub promoter (Robert Armstrong) to bring Joe to Hollywood to star in one of his shows. The show is a success, but Joe is unhappy. Audience members sneak Joe alcohol, which makes him drunk and causes him to go on a

BACK TO THE ISLAND

At Comic-Con 2014, the head of Legendary Pictures screened a short clip of test footage for *Skull Island*, the first film attempt to reboot the King Kong franchise since Peter Jackson's 2005 film. The finished film will be a King Kong origin story. An origin story fills in the history or background of an existing movie or character. *Skull Island* will explore the mysterious place King Kong came from.

rampage. A court orders Joe to be put down, and Young must help him make a daring escape back to Africa.

Many of the same people who worked on the 1933 *King Kong* worked on *Mighty Joe Young*, including director Ernest Schoedsack, producer Merian C. Cooper, screenwriter Ruth Rose, and star Robert Armstrong. Willis O'Brien headed the special-effects team, which created more advanced stop-motion animation than was possible in *King Kong*.

Mighty Joe Young was not a box-office smash, but it did win an Academy Award for Best Visual Effects. The movie was remade in 1998 as a Disney family film.

Congo was a 1995 Paramount jungle movie that was based on the novel by Michael Crichton. It is about the mysterious disappearance of a scientific team in a remote part of the Congo and the expedition sent to find out what happened. Along the way, they search for the Lost City of Zinj, where there is supposed to be a diamond mine guarded by killer gorillas. The team finds everything they are looking for, but each member has a different motive, making the expedition even more dangerous than anyone had anticipated.

Congo was a box-office hit but suffered from negative reviews. Critics were disappointed that the gorillas were obviously puppets or people in gorilla costumes. There had been plans to make computer-generated gorillas, but the technology of the time could not produce realistic-looking fur. Advances in technology solved this problem by the time Peter Jackson filmed *King Kong*.

Monstrous apes are a constant theme in B movies. These cheaply produced flicks are often short on plot and have low-priced special effects. They focus on getting apes whipped up into an angry rampage rather than having any real narrative. These films have their fans in people who enjoy silly, sometimes violent movies. A few notable monstrous ape B movies include *The Ape* (1940), *The Ape Man* (1943), *White Pongo* (1945), *Konga* (1961), *The Mighty Gorga* (1969), and *Ape* (1976).

THE *PLANET OF THE APES* FRANCHISES

Unlike some portrayals of King Kong, the intelligent apes in the *Planet of the Apes* movies are not portrayed as mindless monsters, and they have thrilled audiences for more than forty years. These movies, which have had three different franchises, are based on a 1963 novel by French author Pierre Boulle. The setting for these stories is a planet where intelligent apes have overthrown and enslaved humans. The movies show the conflicts between these two groups. Filmmakers have intended for these conflicts to be taken both at face value and as a comment on issues such as the Cold War and racism.

The first franchise began in 1968 with *Planet of the Apes*, followed by *Beneath the Planet of the Apes* (1970), *Escape from the Planet of the Apes* (1971), *Conquest of the Planet of the Apes* (1972), and *Battle for the Planet of the Apes* (1973). This franchise was also spun off into a fourteen-episode

In this scene from **Planet of the Apes** *(1968), the captured astronaut George Taylor (Charlton Heston,* **right***) is being observed by chimpanzee scientists.*

primetime television series that aired in 1974 and a thirteen-episode animated series that aired in 1975.

The first movie is set in the future and stars Charlton Heston as George Taylor, an astronaut who travels to the mysterious planet. Kim Hunter and Roddy McDowall play Zira and Cornelius, respectively, two apes who help Taylor. Maurice Evans plays the ape villain Dr. Zaius. *Planet of the Apes* was a critical and box-office hit and even earned an honorary Oscar for makeup.

Beneath the Planet of the Apes features a similar story and much of the same cast. It was a box-office hit, but critics have called it one of the worst of this series. *Escape from the Planet of the Apes* sends Zira and Cornelius back in time (to the present), where they must deal with people who fear the apes' existence will destroy the human race. This movie did well with critics and at the box office. In *Conquest of the Planet of the Apes*, McDowall plays Cornelius's son Caesar, who leads an uprising against the humans who have enslaved him and his fellow apes. The movie was modestly successful and received mixed reviews, so it was decided to end the series with one last film. *Battle for the Planet of the Apes* follows Caesar after the uprising of the previous film, ending the series on a low note as it was the lowest-earning and worst-reviewed movie in the series.

Director Tim Burton attempted to reimagine the franchise for his 2001 version of *Planet of the Apes* for Fox. In this version, astronaut Leo Davidson (Mark Wahlberg) reaches a distant planet where apes have enslaved humans, and he leads an uprising against the apes. The film was successful at the box office, and while some critics praised the special effects, most felt the storytelling fell short of the original. Because of the movie's mixed reception, Fox decided not to make a sequel.

In 2011, *Rise of the Planet of the Apes* rebooted the franchise once more. It reimagines Caesar's story from *Conquest of the Planet of the Apes*. Here, Caesar has been raised by humans and given a drug that gives him human intelligence. After he is imprisoned in a primate sanctuary,

Rise of the Planet of the Apes *(2011) rebooted the* **Planet of the Apes** *series by exploring Caesar's backstory leading up to the ape uprising. The scene shown here is of Caesar's gorilla ally attacking a helicopter.*

he uses his intelligence to lead an ape uprising. Andy Serkis plays Caesar. He and other ape characters were filmed using motion-capture technology like that used in Peter Jackson's *King Kong*. *Rise of the Planet of the Apes* was a hit with both audiences and critics, leading to a sequel, *Dawn of the Planet of the Apes* (2014). Set ten years later, at a time when a strain of flu has killed off most humans, Caesar and his fellow apes are drawn into a war with the surviving humans in this movie.

It wowed critics and audiences once again with its gripping story and special effects. The series is ongoing, with another installment planned for 2016.

A POP-CULTURE ICON

King Kong is a pop-culture icon. One big ape has unleashed all manner of monstrous apes in every imaginable medium. Many of these apes have become iconic in their own right. Whether you prefer the big screen or the small screen, cutting-edge or camp, there is a King Kong or monstrous ape that will appeal to you.

FILMOGRAPHY

King Kong (1933)
Directors: Merian C. Cooper and Ernest B. Schoedsack
Actors: Fay Wray, Robert Armstrong, and Bruce Cabot

Son of Kong (1933)
Director: Ernest B. Schoedsack
Actors: Robert Armstrong, Helen Mack, and Frank Reicher

The Ape (1940)
Director: William Nigh
Actors: Boris Karloff, Maris Wrixon, Gene O'Donnell, and Dorothy Vaughn

The Ape Man (1943)
Director: William Beaudine
Actors: Bela Lugosi, Louise Currie, Wallace Ford, and Henry Hall

White Pongo (1945)
Director: Sam Newfield
Actors: Richard Fraser, Maris Wrixon, Lionel Royce, and Ray Corrigan

Mighty Joe Young (1949)
Director: Ernest B. Schoedsack
Actors: Terry Moore, Ben Johnson, Robert Armstrong, and Joe Young

Konga (1961)
Director: John Lemont
Actors: Michael Gough, Margo Johns, Jess Conrad, and Paul Stockman

King Kong vs. Godzilla (1962)
Director: Ishiro Honda
Actors: Tadao Takashima, Kenji Sahara, Yû Fujiki, and Shôichi Hirose

King Kong Escapes (1967)
Director: Ishiro Honda
Actors: Rhodes Reason, Mie Hama, Linda Miller, Shôichi Hirose, and Haruo Nakajima

The Mighty Gorga (1969)
Director: David L. Hewitt
Actors: Anthony Eisley, Meghan Timothy, Scott Brady, and David L. Hewitt

Ape (1976)
Director: Paul Leder
Actors: Rod Arrants, Joanna Kerns, Alex Nicol, and Nak-Hun Lee

King Kong (1976)
Director: John Guillermin
Actors: Jeff Bridges, Charles Grodin, Jessica Lange, and Rick Baker

King Kong Lives (1986)
Director: John Guillermin
Actors: Peter Elliot, George Yiasomi, Brian Kerwin, and Linda Hamilton

Congo (1995)
Director: Frank Marshall
Actors: Laura Linney, Dylan Walsh, Ernie Hudson, and Tim Curry

King Kong (2005)
Director: Peter Jackson
Actors: Naomi Watts, Jack Black, Adrien Brody, and Andy Serkis

GLOSSARY

B MOVIE A movie that is cheaply made and that is not considered to be very good.

CAMP/CAMPY Something that is so exaggerated or absurd that its weirdness is entertaining.

CLIMAX The most exciting or important part of a movie. The climax usually happens near the end of the film.

COLLABORATIVE Describes creating something by having teams of people work on it.

DOCUMENTARY A movie that tells the facts about real people, places, or events.

EXOTIC Something unusual that comes from a faraway place.

FRANCHISE A movie series that is built from a single story or idea. *The Planet of the Apes* movies are an example of a franchise.

GENRE A category of movie or other artistic form. Mystery is a movie genre.

GREAT DEPRESSION The global economic downturn that lasted from 1929 to 1939.

IMPROVISED Performed something without preparation or a script.

MATTE A large painted background used in filmmaking.

MOTION-CAPTURE TECHNOLOGY A special-effects technology in which an actor's movements are digitally recorded and then translated into computer-animated images.

SENSOR A device that responds to heat, light, sound, pressure, magnetism, or motion and transmits the resulting impulses to a computer.

STOP-MOTION ANIMATION A special-effects technique in which objects such as clay models are photographed in a series of slightly different positions so that the objects seem to move.

FOR MORE INFORMATION

American Film Institute

2021 N. Western Avenue

Los Angeles, CA 90027-1657

(323) 856-7600

Website: http://afi.com

The American Film Institute seeks to preserve historical motion pictures and to honor the contributions of people in all areas of moviemaking.

Canada Science and Technology Museum

1867 St. Laurent Boulevard

Ottawa, ON K1G 5A3

Canada

(613) 991-3044

Website: http://cstmuseum.techno-science.ca/en

The Canada Science and Technology Museum has a collection dedicated to motion pictures and film technology.

The Museum of the Moving Image

36-01 35 Avenue

Astoria, NY 11106

(718) 784 0077

Website: http://www.movingimage.us

The Museum of the Moving Image promotes the study and enjoyment of the history, technology, and art of moviemaking and television production.

National Film Preservation Board

Library of Congress

Motion Picture, Broadcasting & Recorded Sound Division

101 Independence Avenue SE

Washington, DC 20540-4690

Website: http://www.loc.gov/rr/mopic

The National Film Preservation Board collects and preserves films.

THEMUSEUM

10 King Street West

Kitchener, ON N2G 1A3

Canada

(519) 749-9387

Website: http://www.themuseum.ca

This museum features a hands-on exhibition on stop-motion animation.

WEBSITES

Because of the changing nature of Internet links, Rosen Publishing has developed an online list of websites related to the subject of this book. This site is updated regularly. Please use this link to access the list:

http://www.rosenlinks.com/GMM/Ape

FOR FURTHER READING

FICTION

Crichton, Michael. *Congo*. New York, NY: Vintage, 2012.

DeVito, Joe, Brad Strickland, and John Michlig. *Kong: King of Skull Island*. Milwaukie, OR: Dark Horse, 2005.

Golden, Christopher, Fran Walsh, Philippa Boyens, Peter Jackson, Merian C. Cooper, and Edgar Wallace. *King Kong*. New York, NY: Pocket Books, 2005.

Lovelace, Delos W., Edgar Wallace, and Merian C. Cooper. *King Kong*. New York, NY: Modern Library, 2005.

NONFICTION

Clutter, Brian Matthew. *Titans of Toho: An Unauthorized Guide to the Godzilla Series and the Rest of Toho's Giant Monster Film Library*. Seattle, WA: Createspace, 2014.

Fiscus, James W. *Meet King Kong*. New York, NY: Rosen Publishing, 2005.

Goldner, Orville, and George Turner. *The Making of King Kong: The Story Behind a Film Classic*. Stamford, CT: Oak Tree Publications, 1975.

Landis, John. *Monsters in the Movies*. New York, NY: DK Publishing, 2011.

Morton, Ray. *King Kong: The History of a Movie Icon from Fay Wray to Peter Jackson*. Montclair, NJ: Applause Theatre and Cinema Books, 2005.

Shephard, Will. *Inside King Kong: A Journal*. Gosport, UK: Chaplin Books, 2014.

Vaz, Mark. *Living Dangerously: The Adventures of Merian C. Cooper, Creator of King Kong*. New York, NY: Villard, 2005.

Wake, Jenny. *The Making of King Kong: The Official Guide to the Motion Picture*. New York, NY: Pocket Books, 2005.

Wray, Fay. *On the Other Hand: A Life Story*. North Pomfret, VT: Trafalgar Square, 1990.

BIBLIOGRAPHY

Dark Horse Comics. "Kong: King of Skull Island." Darkhorse.com. Retrieved November 6, 2014 (http://www.darkhorse.com/ Books/10-749/Kong-King-of-Skull-Island-TPB).

Ebert, Roger. "Great Movies: King Kong." Rogerebert.com. February 3, 2002. Retrieved November 4, 2014 (http://www.rogerebert.com/ reviews/great-movie-king-kong-1933).

King, Susan. "Classic Hollywood: 80th Birthday Toast to King Kong." *Los Angeles Times*, February 17, 2013. Retrieved November 3, 2013 (http://articles.latimes.com/2013/feb/17/entertainment/la -et-mn-king-kong-classic-hollywood-20130218).

Morton, Ray. *King Kong: The History of a Movie Icon from Fay Wray to Peter Jackson*. Montclair, NJ: Applause Theatre and Cinema Books, 2005.

Peary, Gerald. "Missing Links: The Jungle Origins of King Kong." *The Girl in the Hairy Paw*. Ronald Gottesman and Harry Geduld, eds., New York, NY: Avon Books, 1976. Retrieved November 4, 2014 (http:// www.geraldpeary.com/essays/jkl/kingkong-1.html).

Rottenberg, Josh. "Return of the Kong." *Entertainment Weekly*, November 18, 2005. Retrieved November 6, 2014 (http://www .ew.com/ew/article/0,,1128298,00.html).

Turner Classic Movies. "King Kong (1933)." Tcm.com. Retrieved November 5, 2014 (http://www.tcm.com/tcmdb/title/2690/King-Kong).

INDEX

ABOUT THE AUTHOR

Jennifer Way is a writer and editor living in northern Virginia with her husband, Dan, and their daughter, June. In her free time, Jennifer enjoys cooking, yoga, and photography.

PHOTO CREDITS

Cover, p. 28 © AF archive/Alamy; p. 4 Mary Evans/Ronald Grant/Everett Collection; pp. 5, 19 courtesy Everett Collection; p. 7 Archive Photos/Moviepix/Getty Images; p. 11 Buyenlarge/Moviepix/Getty Images; p. 14 © Photos 12/Alamy; p. 17 Photofest; p. 22 Michael Ochs Archives/Moviepix/Getty Images; p. 25 © Moviestore collection Ltd/Alamy; p. 27 © Everett Collection Inc/Alamy; p. 30 © United Archives GmbH/Alamy; p. 32 Scott Barbour/Getty Images; p. 36 © Ronald Grant Archive/Alamy; p. 38 © 20th Century Fox Film Corp. All rights reserved/courtesy Everett Collection; pp. 40–41 Andrey_Kuzmin/Shutterstock.com; interior pages banners and backgrounds Nik Merkulov/Shutterstock.com, Apostrophe/Shutterstock.com.

Designer: Brian Garvey; Executive Editor: Hope Lourie Killcoyne